Family Poems

Us

One, Dad;
Two, Mum;
Three, me;
Four, Tom.
Five, Gran;
Six, Gramp;
Seven, dog
Called Tramp.
Eight, cat
Called Puss;
No more,
That's Us.

Eric Finney

If you enjoy *Family Poems*, then why not try
Pet Poems, Animal Poems, School Poems
and *Magic Poems*, also compiled
by Jennifer Curry?

Family Poems

Compiled by

Jennifer Curry

Illustrated by

Sarah Nayler

■SCHOLASTIC

This book is dedicated, with my love,
to all "THE STARS" in my own special family
— Laura, Ruth, Rose, Mark, Peter, Emma and Katie

Scholastic Children's Books,
Commonwealth House, 1–19 New Oxford Street,
London, WC1A 1NU, UK
a division of Scholastic Ltd
London ~ New York ~ Toronto ~ Sydney ~ Auckland
Mexico City ~ New Delhi ~ Hong Kong

Published in the UK by Scholastic Ltd, 2002

ISBN 0 439 99352 0

Printed and bound in Great Britain by Cox & Wyman Ltd, Reading, Berks.

2 4 6 8 10 9 7 5 3 1

CONTENTS

Snapshots   33

Loads and Loads of Love

Snapshots   49

Dribbly-Wibbly Kisses

Snapshots

Quite a Rave

Snapshots

Do Not Catapult the Carrots!

Snapshots

Our Bumper Boonzer Breakaway

Snapshots

I Am the One

Last Word

The Palindromes

Mr and Mrs Palindrome
Live in a house on a hill:
There's Mum and Dad
And Nan and Bob
And Anna and Eve and Lil.
There's Otto the dog
And Pip the pup
And black cats Viv and Ziz:
There's something strange
About their names . . .
I wonder what it is.

Eric Finney

Snapshots

Families come in many guises,
Many shapes and many sizes.

Such a Busy Family

Check the Board!

We're such a busy family
We have to keep a list
Pinned on the kitchen notice board
To make sure nothing's missed.

On Mondays Jack's got swimming,
On Tuesdays I've got dance,
Then later I've got keyboard
And Mel's got flute (advanced).

On Wednesdays Mel and I stay on
To practise the school play
While mum takes Jack to judo
With his best friend, Timmy Ray.

On Thursdays there's just guides and cubs
And Fridays are quite slack
But this week there's Kay's party
(Only ten miles there and back)

Saturdays it's gym and skating,
Football Club for Jack.
What a squash with all mum's shopping
Crammed into the back!

On Sundays mum takes Mel to choir
And drops me off for riding,
Then checks Dad has the dinner on
And isn't busy skiving.

But this week we're in trouble –
Mum's nowhere to be seen.
Her note said "Relaxation Course".
I think that's really mean!

Patricia Leighton

Fall Out

Our dad built us a tree house.
It was really like no other.
We played there many happy hours – till

                    I

                f
                    e
                        l
                            l

                        o
                            u
                                t

                                w
                                    i
                                        t
                                            h

                                        m
                                            y

                                            b
                                                r
                                                    o
                                                        t
                                                            h
                                                                e
                                                                    r

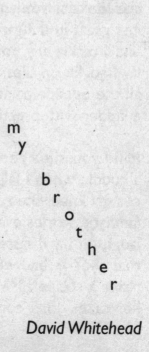

David Whitehead

15

One Parent Family

My mum says she's clueless
not, as you'd imagine,
at wiring three pin plugs or
straightening a bicycle wheel,
but at sewing buttons
on a shirt, icing names and
dates on birthday cakes,
preparing a three-course meal.

She's not like other mothers;
although she's slim and neat
she looks silly in an apron,
just great in dungarees.
She'll tackle any household job,
lay lino, fix on tiles, does
all the outside paintwork, climbs
a ladder with practised ease.

Mind you, she's good for
a cuddle when I fall and
cut my knee. She tells me
fantastic stories every night,
laughs at *my* disasters, says
that she's as bad when she
reads a recipe all wrong and
her cakes don't come out right.

I know on Open Evenings
she gives a bad impression
at the school. She doesn't wear
the proper clothes. "Too bad,"
the others sometimes say,
"you've got such a peculiar mum."
"It's just as well," I tell them.
"She is my mother *and* my dad!"

Moira Andrew

Clickerty-Clackerty
High-Heel Song

My sister's shoes go down the street,
clickerty-clackerty on her feet,
high-heeled shoes that hurt her toes,
clickerty-clackerty there she goes,
leather shoes that slip and slide,
clickerty-clackerty slim not wide,
polished shoes that shine all night,
clickerty-clackerty red and white,
high-heeled shoes will not last long,
clickerty-clackerty that's their song,
my sister's shoes tap out this beat,
clickerty-clackerty on her feet.

Moira Clark

Mothers' Day

We really tried to spoil our Mum
On Mothers' Day:
Took her breakfast up to bed
On a tray;
Gave her presents, cards and flowers –
A lovely bunch;
Did the washing up and cleaning,
Cooked the lunch.
Housework? We wouldn't let her
Lift a finger;
Put a CD on of Frank,
Her favourite singer.
We made the whole day for our Mum
A real treat,
With lots of lovely things
To drink and eat.
Mum thanked us all and said,
"Today was bliss!
Could you please arrange for every day
To be like this?"

Eric Finney

A Thoroughly Modern Grandmama

I've become a world authority
on how grandmothers *ought* to look
because dotty dear old ladies
smile from every picture book.

They're usually round and cuddly
with grey hair and a hat.
They drink endless cups of milky tea,
always, always have a cat.

They're very good at knitting,
and they'll mind you for the day –
I'm sure picture book grannies are
all very well, but boring in their way.

Now *my* grandmother hasn't read
the books – she hasn't got a clue
about the way she should behave
and the things she mustn't do.

She's always on a diet
and I'm sure she dyes her hair,
and I haven't got a grandpapa so
her boyfriend's sometimes there.

She wears jazzy shirts and skin-tight
jeans, jangles bracelets on her arm.
She zooms me around in her little car,
strapped-in, and safe from harm.

She's a busy lady with a job
and a diary to book me in.
She doesn't knit and doesn't drink tea,
preferring coffee, wine or gin!

My grandmother's a complete disaster
as ordinary grannies go —
but I wouldn't want to swap her
or I'd have done it long ago!

Moira Andrew

Granny Granny Please Comb My Hair

Granny Granny
please comb my hair
you always take your time
you always take such care

You put me to sit on a cushion
between your knees
you rub a little coconut oil
parting gentle as a breeze

Mummy Mummy
she's always in a hurry – hurry
rush
she pulls my hair
sometimes she tugs

But Granny
you have all the time in the world
and when you're finished
you always turn my head and say
"Now who's a nice girl."

Grace Nichols

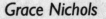

A Step-Ladder

before I go dizzy!

so stop this ladder

my brain's turning frizzy

There are so many steps

and one other floor.

steps up to the landing

right up to the door

The house has steps

three step-rats.

twenty step-fish

two step-cats

four step-dogs

mostly step can'ts

some step cans

three step-aunts

a step-grandma

and several others

one step-sister

two step-brothers

I've got → a new step-dad

Laurelle Rond

23

Snapshots

First meet the babies, gummy and gooey,
Sometimes wet and *often* pooey.

Birth of a Baby

January 16th, 1991,
Was all set to be an ordinary day,
But the ringing of the phone at seven thirty
Changed that.
For nine months
My step mum had carried a load,
Nine months of feeling
Like a beached whale.
That Wednesday,
Bethany Clare was born.
It was my dad on the phone,
Telling the good news,
"Mother and baby both fit and well."
That night I went to visit.
She was so small,
So delicate,
So harmless.
I held her;
She is beautiful,
My half sister.

Gemma Chilvers (13)

The Naming Ceremony

Her name sounds like water, like waves on the
　　sea,
like a summer breeze in the tallest tree.
　　Ashanti, Ashanti, Ashanti.

Her dad is black, her mum is white.
They said, "Please wear something bright."
　　For Ashanti, Ashanti, Ashanti.

We made a great circle under the sun.
Some poems were read, some songs were sung.
　　To Ashanti, Ashanti, Ashanti.

We rattled our shakers, made music with bells.
A storyteller told tales, cast good African spells.
　　Over Ashanti, Ashanti, Ashanti.

They blessed her, sprinkling her face with water,
said a prayer of thanks for their little daughter.
　　Our Ashanti, Ashanti, Ashanti.

Her black grandfather then planted a tree.
Her white grandma held her up for all to see.
　　Ashanti, Ashanti, Ashanti.

She was passed like a parcel in a party game,
as each whispered in turn her beautiful name.
Ashanti, Ashanti, Ashanti.

Moira Andrew

For Sale

One baby (girl) almost brand new.
No teeth yet –
but first one coming through.
High on screams and yells
(better than six alarm bells!)
Fills nappies for England
(six a day as a rule)
but good feet for a girl
(kicks like a mule).

Comes complete with
assorted frocks
babygrows
frilly socks
one box of toys
and a carry cot.

£10 or nearest offer
(or free to a *really far away* home).
Phone 0123 456
and ask for Tommy Briggs.
If a grown-up answers
PUT THE PHONE DOWN QUICK
(and try again later).

Patricia Leighton

Leaky Baby

Our brand new baby's sprung a leak!
He's dripping like a spout.
We'd better send him back
Before the guarantee runs out.

Kaye Umansky

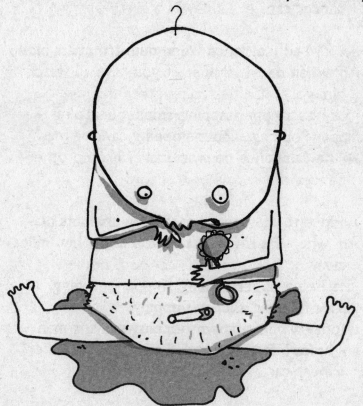

Rap-a-Bye Baby

Ali love to tap-dance when dem drums all beat,
An' when dat rhythm start you never catch
   those feet
'cos he's a tipper-tapping, snipper-snapping
   dancing man
an' he can dance de world away like no other
   dancer can.

Ali love to tap-dance when dem trumpets blow,
An' when dat rhythm start you have to watch
   him go
'cos he's a tipper-tapping, snipper-snapping
flipper-flopping, slipper-slopping dancing man
an' he can dance de world away like no other
   dancer can.

Ali love to tap-dance when dem clarinets play,
An' when dat rhythm start you know him miles
   away
'cos he's a tipper-tapping, snipper-snapping,
flipper-flopping, slipper-slopping,
clapper-clipping, bipper-bopping dancing man
an' he can dance de world away like no other
   dancer can.

He can dance de world away like no other dancer
  can;
he can dance de world away although he only in his
  pram!

Judith Nicholls

Potting Peter

We're potty training Peter,
Mum wants to get him dry.
We rush him to the potty
Each time we hear him cry.

Then little Peter sits and smiles
And looks serenely happy,
But when his mother dresses him,
He grins and wets his nappy.

David Whitehead

Snapshots

Then mum and dad, sisters and brothers,
Grans and grandads ... plus a few others.

Loads and Loads of Love

My Hero

*Dad, dad, there's a monster
under my bed!*
I yelled down the stairs.
   Give it a pat on the head,
   dad shouted up.
   And get back to bed.

*Dad, dad, there's a vampire bat
battering down
the window pane!*
   Not that old thing again.
   Tell it it's got the wrong house,
   dad said.
   And get back to bed.

*Dad, dad, there's a ghost
moaning and groaning
in the wardrobe
trying to get out!*
   Probably fancies watching TV
   Tell it there's nothing good on.
   And get back to bed
   dad said.

Dad, DAD, there's a horrible
hairy black spider
dangling from the ceiling.
It's heading for ME!
Dad dashed up the stairs.
Quick as a flash
the spider
was in his hands
and flushed down the bath.

There, there, pet,
nothing to be scared of now.
he said.
I'll stay with you.
Hop into bed.

Patricia Leighton

A Card For Fathers' Day

Let's make a card for Dad
With pictures of things he likes:
Mum and all of us, of course,
And cars and motor-bikes.

Books, CDs and hi-fi,
Models of sailing ships,
Trees and flowers and gardens,
Bacon, egg and chips.

Write our names inside it —
And what shall we write above?
TO THE SUNNIEST, FUNNIEST
DAD IN THE WORLD,
WITH LOADS AND LOADS OF LOVE.

Eric Finney

My Brother Barry

He thinks he's a cool dude
In his winklepicker boots
And black leather coat.
His dark spiked hair
Makes him look like a hedgehog,
Red spots spangle
His chubby cheeks,
Everyone knows him better by
Monto.
He has a tough walk,
And an awkward run,
Always has three girlfriends
Not one.
You'd hear his car
In Timbucktoo
When he starts it in the morning,
He's no Elvis,
But to me, he's a star.

Glenn Montgomery (10)

Missing Mum

Mum's missing.
Now it's our Dad
reading stories.
Kissing goodnight.

He takes us to
school – my brother
and me. Cooks
us our tea.

He didn't say
why she went away,
or when she'd be
back. Not today.

Not tomorrow.
His face, full of
sorrow when he
said she'd phone.

She's found a new
home where we
can visit. But
that's no good.

Is it?
Mum's still missing.
And we're
missing Mum.

Ann Bonner

Stepmother

My Stepmother
   is really nice.
She ought to wear
   a label.
I don't come in
   with a latch key, now –
my tea is on
   the table.
She doesn't nag at me
   or shout.
I often hear her
   singing.
I'm glad my dad
   had wedding bells –
and I hope
   they go on ringing.

Stepmothers
   in fairy tales
are hard and cold
   as iron.
There isn't a lie
   they wouldn't tell,
or a trick
   they wouldn't try on.

But MY stepmother's
   warm and true;
she's kind and cool,
   and clever –
Yes! I've a *wicked*
   stepmother –
and I hope she stays
   for ever!

Jean Kenward

My Aunt

Tight squeezer
Lipstick smudger
Story teller
Plant lover
Fast knitter
Baby-sitter
Bus rider
Soap watcher
Tea drinker
Tea dancer
Old swinger
Day tripper
Letter writer
Kind thinker
Treat bringer
Real spoiler.

Coral Rumble

In Praise of Aunties

An aunt
is a tender plant.
You really can't
be too fond of an aunt.

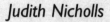

Judith Nicholls

My Gran

My Gran is
    a giggle-in-the-corner-like-a-child
            kind of Gran

She is
    a put-your-cold-hand-in-my-pocket
    a keep-your-baby-curls-in-my-locket
            kind of Gran

She is
    a make-it-better-with-a-treacle-toffee
    a what-you-need's-a-cup-of-milky-coffee
    a hurry-home-I-love-you-awfully
            kind of Gran

She is
    a butter-ball-for-your-bad-throat
    a stitch-your-doll-a-new-green-coat
    a let's-make-soapy-bubbles-float
    a hold-my-hand-I'm-seasick-in-a-boat
            kind of Gran

She is
   a toast-your-tootsies-by-the-fire
   a crack-the-wishbone-for-your-heart's-desire
   a ladies-don't-sweat-they-perspire
   a funny-old-fashioned-higgeldy-piggeldy-lady-to-admire
               kind of Gran

And this lovely grandmother
   is mine, all mine!

Moira Andrew

Until Gran Died

The minnows I caught
lived for a few days in a jar
then floated side-up on the surface.
We buried them beneath the hedge.
I didn't cry, but felt sad inside.

I thought
I could deal with funerals
that is until Gran died.

The goldfish I kept in a bowl
passed away with old age.
Mum wrapped him in newspaper
and we buried him next to a rose bush.
I didn't cry, but felt sad inside.

I thought
I could deal with funerals
that is until Gran died.

My cat lay stiff in a shoe box
after being hit by a car.
Dad dug a hole and we buried her
under the apple tree.
I didn't cry, but felt *very* sad inside.

I thought
I could deal with funerals
that is until Gran died.

And when she died
I went to the funeral
with relations dressed in black.
They cried, and so did I.
Salty tears ran down my face. Oh, how I cried.

Yes, I thought
I could deal with funerals,
that is until Gran died.

She was buried in a graveyard
and even the sky wept that day.
Rain fell and fell and fell,
and thunder sobbed far away
  across the town.
I cried and I cried.

I thought
I could deal with funerals,
that is until Gran
died.

Wes Magee

Seeing All My Family

Seeing all my family
together
at special occasions
is a brilliant firework show
going off.

Grandma is a sparkler,
Grandad is golden rain
making us brighter.
My cousins
are Catherine Wheels.
My dad is a banger
because he always talks too loud.
The best one of all
that lights up the sky
so everyone stares
is my mum,
the incredible blast of sparkle,
the rocket.

Every time we meet
it always has the same effect,
our family firework show.

Claire Salama (10)

there's mum

Snapshots

I'm glad they're there. If they weren't I'd miss them
But why? oh why? do we have to *kiss* them?

Dribbly-Wibbly Kisses

Noisy Feast

Want to eat you up, gobble you up, cuddle you up, spread you on toast
Want to give you nips, slurp my lips, waggle your hips, love you the most
Want to wobble you like jelly, blow raspberries on your belly, smiley and smelly, put you in a pie
Want to wiggle your knee, eat you for tea, squeeze you to me, my baby, the apple of my eye

Laurelle Rond

Home-Time

She's always there
waiting at the gate,
with her welcoming smile.
She's never late.

She watches me
as I run outside.
Her eyes light up,
her arms open wide.

There's just one thing
that spoils all this. . .
Please Mum, *don't* give me
a big sloppy K I S S!

(Well, not in front of my mates, anyway.)

Tracey Blance

Kisses!

Last week
my face was smothered in kisses.
Yes – KISSES!

First there was the dribbly-wibbly kiss
when Mum slurped all over me
like an eight mouthed octopus. ("There's my
   favourite boy!")
Then there was the lipstick-redstick kiss
when my aunty's rosy lips
painted themselves on my cheeks. ("Isn't he so
   handsome!")
Next came the flutter-eye, butterfly kiss
when my girlfriend smoochy-cooched
and fluttered her eyelashes at the same time.
   ("OOOOOOOOH!")
After that there was the soggy-doggy kiss
when our pet Labrador Sally
tried to lick my face off. ("Slop! Slop! Woof!")
Following that there was "watch out here I
   come" miss-kiss
when my little sister aimed for me
but missed and kissed the cat instead.
   ("UUUUUUUUURGH!")

Then there was the spectacular-Dracula kiss
when my cousin Isabel leapt from behind the
   shower curtain
and attacked my neck. ("AAAAAAAAAAGH –
   suck!")
Of course, there was the "sssssssssh don't tell
   anyone" self-kiss
when I looked in the bathroom mirror
and kissed myself. (Once was enough!)

But the unbeatable, second to none, zing-dinger
   of a kiss
came from Gran.
It was a lipsucking, cheek plucking, Donald Ducking,
SMACKEROONY OF A KISS. (She's forgotten
   to put her teeth in!)

Ian Souter

uck..
I

Hugger Mugger

I'd sooner be
Jumped and thumped and dumped

I'd sooner be
Slugged and mugged ... than *hugged*...

And clobbered with a slobbering
Kiss by Auntie Jean:

You know what I mean:

Whenever she comes to stay,
You know you're bound

To get one.
A quick
    short
    peck
    would
    be
    OK
But this is a
Whacking great
Smacking great
Wet one!

All whoosh and spit
And crunch and squeeze
And "*Dear* little boy!"
And "Auntie's missed you!"
And "Come to Auntie, she
Hasn't *kissed* you!"
Please don't do it, Auntie,
PLEASE!
Or if you've absolutely
Got to,

And nothing on *earth* can persuade you
Not to,

The trick
Is to make it
Quick,

You know what I mean?

For as things are,
I really would far,

Far sooner be
Jumped and thumped and dumped,

I'd sooner be
Slugged and mugged . . . than *hugged*. . .

And clobbered with a slobbering
Kiss by my Auntie
Jean!

Kit Wright

Squeezes

We love to squeeze bananas,
We love to squeeze ripe plums,
And when they are feeling sad
We love to squeeze our mums.

Brian Patten

When I'm on My Own

When I'm on my own,
I feel cold
like a block of ice.
But
when I have a hug
from my mum
I melt.

Alice Aldous (8)

My Little Sister

My little sister
doesn't kick, or thump, or scratch, or slog you,
my little sister
just wants to snog you...

And if you're not quick to escape
she'll nab you.
she'll take you by surprise
and grab you...

And it isn't a peck on the neck
or the briefest brush of the lips.

She's an artist who likes
to paint your face

with a sliding kiss
that seems like a snail
has left its trail on your cheek!

Brian Moses

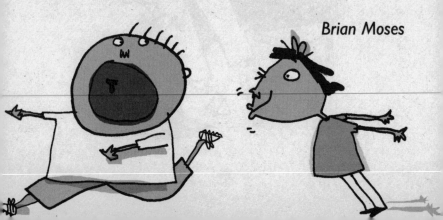

Snapshots

And the jobs they give us! You wouldn't believe it!
Wash it! Dry it! Tidy and clear it!

Tidy Your Room Now!

A Kid's Life

L.A.U.R.A.A.A.A.A.!
Get upstairs and tidy your room NOW!
Don't do that,
Leave him alone,
Stop picking your nose,
Clean your teeth,
How dare you,
Eat your dinner,
Do your homework,
Go to bed,
Get up,
Get off that computer NOW!
Hurry up,
Switch the telly off,
Lay the table,
Wash up,
Make your bed,
Feed the rabbits,
Don't be stupid,
Don't be rude,

Naughty girl,
Don't fluffle the dogs at the table,
NO!
YES!
I DON'T KNOW!
DON'T ASK ME!
Go away!
Bring your washing down,
Come on,
Don't be such a pain,
Go and give this to the goat,
Why are you always so difficult?

Laura Maskell (11)

It's Really Not Deliberate!

It's really not deliberate
That every day I drop a plate
Or cup or mug – *they slip and smash*
As carefully the stuff I wash.

Dad moaned our twenty four piece set
Had reached, at last count, ninety eight!
Oh whoops – there goes another – CRASH
It's really not deliberate!

I don't know why they don't ask Kate
Instead of getting in a state –
I know it's costing tons of cash
And Kate I'm sure won't make a hash.
Though washing up's a job I HATE ...
It's *really* NOT deliberate!

Philip Waddell

Harry Pushed Her

Harry pushed her;
He pushed her around;
He pushed his sister.
Before school, after school;
On weekends.
He pushed his sister;
He had no friends.
He pushed her: school holidays
And Christmas time.
The children always
Sang their made-up rhyme:
"Harry push her! Push her quick!
Harry push her! Make her sick!"
Harry pushed her without strain:
Through snow, sunshine, wind and rain.
She smiled strangely
And never said a word.
He pushed her for years –
It was so absurd.
Harry was twelve;
His sister twenty-three.
Harry never had a childhood like me.
Harry pushed her without a care;
He pushed his sister in her wheelchair.

Peter Thabit Jones

My Brother

My brother comes in and says:
"Tell him to clear the fluff
out from under his bed."
Mum says,
"Clear the fluff
out from under your bed."
Father says,
"You heard what your mother said."
"What?" I say.
"The fluff," he says.
"Clear the fluff
out from under your bed."
So I say,
"There's fluff under his bed, too,
you know."
So father says,
"But we're talking about the fluff
under *your* bed."
"You will clear it up
won't you?" Mum says.
So now my brother – all puffed up –
says,
"Clear the fluff
out from under your bed,
clear the fluff
out from under your bed."

Now I'm angry. I am angry.
So I say – what shall I say?
I say,
"Shuttup Stinks
YOU CAN'T RULE MY LIFE."

Michael Rosen

Mothers Who Don't Understand

"Why can't you tidy your room?" they cry,
Millions of mothers who fret round the land,
"It's a horrible mess, I've never seen worse,"
– Mothers who don't understand.

They don't understand how cosy it is
To have piles of books on the floor,
And knickers and socks making friends with the
   vest
Under the bed, where they like it best,
And notices pinned to the door.

They don't understand why Kylie and Craig
Are smiling all over the walls,
And toffees and Chewys and dozens of Smarties
Are scattered about reminding of parties,
And jeans are rolled into balls.

They don't understand why a good bed should be
All scrumpled and friendly and gritty,
Why the bears and the paints and the toys are
   much less
Easy to find if there isn't a mess –
To tidy would be a great pity.

They don't understand the point of a desk
Is to balance the muddle quite high:
To leave the drawers open, grow mould on the drink,
Is very much easier, some people think,
Than explaining to mothers just why.

"PLEASE can you tidy your room?" they wail,
Millions of mothers who fret round the land:
"What will you do when there's no one to nag you?"
– Mothers who don't understand.

Augusta Skye

Questions

Who likes to swing from
The branch of a tree?

I DO!

Who likes cheeseburgers
With baked beans for tea?

I DO!

Who likes to watch
What comes on the TV?

I DO!

Who likes to tidy up my bedroom,
Fetch the shopping,
Cook the lunch
And do the washing up?

MUM DOES!

Doesn't she. . . ?

Trevor Harvey

Snapshots

Sometimes we get mad (a bit!)
But when we do, they throw a fit.

Gnrr.

I Put My Tongue Out

Steaming!

I was a slouch on a couch,
watching a favourite TV programme,
when my sister rolled into our lounge
like a gunslinger looking for trouble.
And **with** a smirk and smile
but **without** a please or a pause
she swaggered over
and simply changed the channels!

Now all day long my sister
had been annoying me.
Filled with devilment,
skilled at annoying,
she thrilled at causing trouble for **me**!
Now here she was – **at it again**
and I'd had enough,
that final snigger had ignited my temper!

Suddenly my anger was a swelling fist,
fire began crackling in my head,
blood began boiling in my brain.
I glared, I stared,
I scowled, I growled.
I wasn't mild – **I was wild!**
I wasn't bad – **I was mad!**
I wasn't dreaming – **I was steaming!**
STEAMING like a train out of control
and just as I was about to derail my temper
my sister smiled knowingly and shouted, **"Mum!"**
And suddenly my anger was braking
my temper was no longer shaking,
my fury was no longer waking
as I realized the risk was not worth taking!
For while my temper is bad
it's not half as wicked
as my **Mum's!**

Ian Souter

Sisters

ssssssssssssss!ssssssssssterssss

sssssssssssssssisssssssssterssssssssss

Gina Douthwaite

Our Mother

Our mother is a detective.
She is a great finder of clues.
She found the mud and grass on our shoes,
When we were told not to go in the park –
Because it would be getting dark –
But come straight home.

She found the jam on our thumbs,
And in our beds the tiniest crumbs,
From the cakes we said we had not eaten.
When we blamed the cat for breaking the fruit
  bowl –
Because we did not want any fuss –
She *knew* it was us.

Allan Ahlberg

Face Pulling Contests

My sister and I
hold face pulling contests.

I start with my
zombie at midnight look
while she hooks two fingers
into her mouth and pulls out
her sabre tooth tiger scowl.

I try my curse
of the killer mummies,
but she rolls her eyes
and curls her lip,
sticks out her teeth
and pretends she's Drac.
I clutch at my throat
and finger a bolt,
then zap her with
Frankenstein's features.

She comes at me
with her wolf woman sneer,
but I can howl
much better than her.
And now she's stuck
for something to do,
and this time I'm thinking
I'll beat her for sure
with my purple planet people eater ...

when Mum steps in
to check the noise,
and no one pulls a better face
than Mum when she's annoyed.

My sister and I
are mere beginners:

Mum's the winner!

Brian Moses

I Put My Tongue Out

I put my tongue out –
Just licking my lips –
But Mum thought I did it
'Cos she'd said, "No more chips!"

I put my tongue out:
It needed some air.
But Mum thought I did it
'Cos she'd said, "Comb your hair."

I put my tongue out
To make sure it was red.
But Dad thought I did it
'Cos he'd said, "Time for bed."

I just put my tongue out –
Is that such a sin?
Maybe next time I'd better
Keep my tongue in.

Eric Finney

Richard's Brother Speaks

Richard...
What's the matter? Why you not smiln' no more?
You wretch, you bruk the window?
Daddy a go peel you 'kin,
'Im a go peel it like how he peel orange.
When Daddy come true dat door.
You better run.
You better leave de country!
'Im a-go peel you 'kin.
You bottom a go warm tonight though!
Me goin' cook dinner pon you backside
When 'im done wid you
Richard 'im a come!
Run, bwoy, run!

Desmond Strachan

Fingerlicking

I went to the kitchen
Find de food finger licking
I tek out a de fridge
A nice big piece a chicken.
I started to nyam it
But me mammy come an grab it
And gimme a piece a licking
And sen me to me bed.

Judith Ellis

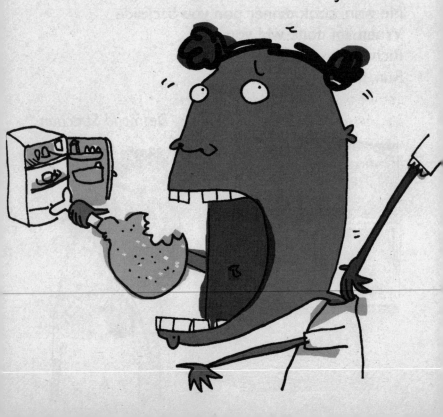

It Isn't Me – Honest

There's someone in our family
who always leaves
the loo seat up,
towels on the floor,
sticky marks on every door,
the top off the toothpaste,
socks on the bed,
tissues in pockets
about to be washed
and red, red felt-tip
on the tablecloth –
it's enough to make
my mum's blood boil
but worst of all
someone in the family
has dared to wipe
his bogies on the wall
behind our leather sofa,
and it isn't me, honest.

Moira Clark

My Family's Sleeping Late Today

My family's sleeping late today,
but I am wide awake,
and making all the racket
it is possible to make.
I'm rapping on a window pane,
I'm hammering a nail,
I'm playing tackle with the cat,
and yanking on her tail.

I'm racing madly through the house,
I'm slamming every door,
I'm imitating jungle sounds,
I trumpet and I roar.
I think I'll play my tambourine
and pop a big balloon,
they'll never sleep through all of that,
they're sure to get up soon.

Jack Prelutsky

The Thing

It lurks beneath the sheets,
this monstrous lump,
with straggly dark hair
poking out in all directions.
I speak to it
from a distance,
it grunts in response.

I tiptoe closer,
and poke it gently,
then quickly retreat.

Suddenly
it E-X-P-L-O-D-E-S,
leaping like a wild animal,
growling, snarling,
gnashing its teeth.

I *knew* I shouldn't have
woken dad so early.

Tracey Blance

I Din Do Nuttin

I din do nuttin
I din do nuttin
I din do nuttin
All I did
was throw Granny pin
in the rubbish bin.

I did do nuttin
I din do nuttin
I din do nuttin
All I did
was mix paint in
Mammy biscuit tin.

I din do nuttin
I din do nuttin.

John Agard

Snapshots

So mostly we chill out, stay cool,
And let the grown-ups play the fool.

Dad

83

Quite a Rave

Beware of the Uncles!

With Uncle Pete and Uncle Dave
today at the fair was quite a rave.
Uncle Dave and Uncle Pete
bought the w i l d e s t things to eat.

Uncle Dave and Uncle Pete
thought roller-coaster rides were neat,
we always got the s c a r i e s t seat.
Then Uncle Pete and Uncle Dave
s c r e a m e d on the train through Dracula's
  Cave.
WE told THEM they had to behave.

Mark Bones

The Spoons Music Man

My Uncle
made music with spoons.

He could play
any number of tunes.

He banged them
on knees and his nose.

He banged them
on elbows and toes.

My Uncle
made wonderful tunes.

He made
magical music with spoons.

Wes Magee

Digital Dad

He's a digital dad,
but he's driving us mad —
keeps hogging the screen.
You know what we mean:
every time, it's the same,
he takes over *our* game
and we can't make a fuss;
he's much better than us!

Mike Johnson

Dad

Football Fever

I've caught football fever
Now I'm football mad
Football's taken over
I've got football bad

Yes, I've got football fever
I thought I was immune
But I'm not *sick as a parrot*
Instead I'm *over the moon*

So I don't need a doctor
I don't need a pill
I'm not feeling awful
I'm not really ill

I've just got football fever
I've just gone football mad
I'm as crazy as my sister
As barmy as my Dad

We've all got football fever
Each one did succumb
But if you think *we've* got it bad
Wait till you meet Mum!

Bernard Young

My Grandpa

My grandpa is as round shouldered
as a question mark
and is led about all day
by his walking stick.
With teeth that aren't real,
hidden behind a moustache that is,
while his memories simmer warmly
inside his crinkled paper bag of a face.

My grandpa,
old and worn on the outside,
sparky and fresh on the in.
For he often,
shakes my hand with fifty pence pieces,
makes sweets pop out from behind his ears,
smokes all day like a train
then laughs like one as well.
Plays jokes on my mother
as he tries to freshen her face with a smile
and then tells me stories that electrify my brain.

But best of all,
when my dad loses his temper,
Grandpa just tells him
to sit down and behave himself!

Good old grandpa!

Ian Souter

Unbelievable

Sleepover!
My very first one.
I'd made it,
was "in" with the gang.
It felt grand.

I'll pack your things,
said mum.
Get some chocolate bars
from the fridge,
a few packets
of crisps.
She's the tops, she is!

Sleeping bags everywhere,
bare feet and bottoms
getting ready for bed.
Gave mine a shake
for my jim-jams
and flushed bright red.
Out shot Floppetty Bunny.
Mum – you're *dead!*

Patricia Leighton

Artificial Hip-Hop

Granny's groovy, Granny's cool,
she runs the discos at my school:
wrinkly reggae, blue-rinse rock,
false-teeth techno. Quite a shock,
she swings her zimmer-frame around:
"DJ Senior Citizen of Sound".
Artificial hip-hop bobbing,
spins like a 12". Never stopping,
turns her hearing-aid to LOUD;
this pensioned-punk makes me feel proud
she runs the discos at my school.
Granny's groovy, Granny's cool.

Mike Johnson

Seven Snowmen

We built seven
Snowmen my
brother and me.
Some of them
had no heads.
Some of them
were fat. Some
of them had
faces, and
some didn't.
All of them
Were different,
But one thing
They were all
Cold. And so
Were we!
My brother
and me.

Vanessa Steele (5)

Snapshots

Breakfast ... dinner ... tea ... – I'd say
Meals are the best times of our day.

Do Not Catapult The Carrots!

A Lesson

Darren took all
the labels off
the tins in Mummy's
shopping bag.

He sorted them
like teacher had,
red and yellow,
green and blue.

Tonight the dog
had soup for tea,
the cat had beans
and Darren had

Whiskas.
He said it
tasted horrible
on toast.

Brian Morse

Baby Breakfast

Squidge
My food in my fist
Throw
It at the wall
Rub
It in my hair
Soak
It in my milk
Squeeze
The dirt out
Stuff
It in my mouth
Splurt
It across the room
Dig
It out of my bib
Catapult
It to Mummy
Aim
It at Daddy
Mmmm
Finished.

Julia Marsden (15)

Give Up Slimming, Mum

My mum
is short
and plump
and pretty
and I wish
she'd give up
slimming.

So does Dad.

Her cooking's
delicious –
you can't
beat it –
but you really can
hardly bear
to eat it –
the way she sits
with her eyes
brimming,
watching you
polish off
the spuds
and trimmings
while she
has nothing
herself but a small
thin dry
diet biscuit;
that's all.

My mum
is short
and plump
and pretty
and I wish
she'd give up
slimming

So does Dad.

She says she
looks as though
someone had
sat on her –
BUT WE LIKE MUM
WITH A BIT
OF FAT ON HER!

Kit Wright

Hot Food

We sit down to eat
and the potato's a bit hot
so I only put a little bit on my fork
and I blow
whooph whooph
until it's cool
just cool
then into the mouth
nice.
And there's my brother
he's doing the same
whooph whooph
into the mouth
nice.
There's my mum
she's doing the same
whooph whooph
into the mouth
nice.
But my dad.
My dad.
What does he do?
He stuffs a great big chunk of potato
into his mouth.
then
that really does it.

His eyes pop out
he flaps his hands
he blows, he puffs, he yells
he bobs his head up and down
he spits bits of potato
all over his plate
and he turns to us and he says,
"Watch out everybody –
the potato's very hot."

Michael Rosen

Going to Tea with Grandma

I'm going to tea with Grandma
I wonder what there'll be?
A big round cake with a cherry on top,
Some biscuits and a cup of tea.

I'm going to tea with Grandma
She asked me what I'd like.
Jelly perhaps and ice-cream too,
Oh what a lovely sight.

I'm going to tea with Grandma
I'll help her make the tea.
Then we'll sit down and eat it all,
Just Grandma and me.

Alexandra Calvert (7)

Good Advice

Wash yuh han dem before yuh eat
Sit still, stop twitching in yuh seat,
Don' bang the plate with yuh knife an fork,
An keep quiet when big people a-talk
Stop drag yuh foot dem pon the floor,
Ah tell yuh a'ready, don' slam the door,
Cover up yuh mout when yuh a cough,
Don' be greedy, give yuh sister half
O' the banana that yuh eating there,
What kind o' dress that yuh a-wear?
Don' hiss yuh teeth when me talk to yuh.
And mind how yuh looking at me too,
Teck me good advice me girl,
Manners carry yuh through the worl',
Ah tellin yuh this fe yuh own good
Yuh should thank me, show me some gratitude.

Life is really tough for me,
When Uncle Henry comes to tea.

Valerie Bloom

My Mother Says I'm Sickening

My mother says I'm sickening,
my mother says I'm crude,
she says this when she sees me
playing Ping-Pong with my food,
she doesn't seem to like it
when I slurp my bowl of stew,
and now she's got a list of things
she says I mustn't do –

DO NOT CATAPULT THE CARROTS!
DO NOT JUGGLE GOBS OF FAT!
DO NOT DROP THE MASHED POTATOES
ON THE GERBIL OR THE CAT!
NEVER PUNCH THE PUMPKIN PUDDING!
NEVER TUNNEL THROUGH THE BREAD!
PUT NO PEAS INTO YOUR POCKET!
PLACE NO NOODLES ON YOUR HEAD!
DO NOT SQUEEZE THE STEAMED ZUCCHINI!
DO NOT MAKE THE MELON OOZE!
NEVER STUFF VANILLA YOGHURT
IN YOUR LITTLE SISTER'S SHOES!

I wish my mother wouldn't make
so many useless rules.

Jack Prelutsky

Grandma's Winter Warmer

Grandma wants a knees-up,
>   she wants to have a ball

The whole street has the breeze-up,
>   and no-one's safe at all.

She says there's been a freeze-up,
>   so we deserve a chance.

Or else her knees will seize-up,
>   if she can't have a dance!

And a cake and beer and cheese-up!
And a jelly and pies and peas-up!
I hope she let's me stay up,
   now that I'm not small.
   I want to see it all.

Mark Bones

Snapshots

And when summer comes, if we go away,
We have brilliant times on our holiday.

Our Bumper Boonzer Breakaway

Postcard

Dear Gran
        I'm at the seaside And it Isn't like I thought In fact this picture postcard Is the only one I've bought. The sand is much too sandy, the sea's not very dry And I haven't seen a mermaid! Home on Saturday. Love, Di xx

Sue Cowling

Recipe for a Disastrous Family Picnic

Ingredients:

2 fed-up parents
1 crying baby
2 arguing children
1 picnic hamper full of sticky goodies
that will attract ants, wasps and hairy things!
1 unreliable car
1 green meadow

What to do:

Place the first four ingredients
and boil in the car for 45 minutes.
Mix in a few arguments,
a change of nappy and a punctured tyre.
Then remove and place on a slice of fresh, green
    meadow.
Next open the picnic hamper
and take out the items.
Set out a blanket or white tablecloth
dropping one or two things as you go!

Slowly add on an army of ants, a few wasps
and of course a stray, hairy dog!
Then wash it all down with a heavy thunderstorm.

Please note that this recipe works best
if served near a herd of cows
and a few fresh cowpats!

Ian Souter

Humph!

Holiday Time – Again

The year's two thousand two hundred
And we're off on a trip to the moon
For our annual family holiday
– last two weeks in June.

Mum's got the latest in spacesuits,
Dad's moon boots are top of the range,
Gran and gramps have matching backpacks
And we don't need to *think* about rain.

Not much to see on the journey,
I'm stuck in the aisle with no view.
It's a good job we'll soon be landing
– Sal's flirting with all of the crew!

Been here a week – it's so boring!
Nothing but crater trips.
Moon buggy hire costs a fortune
And the lunar canteen's got no chips.

Mum's getting humpy and grumpy,
Dad's running low on cash,
Gran and gramps want "*a good cup of tea*"
And Sal has come out in a rash.

Still, next year should be quite different.
I'm thanking my lucky stars
I'll be old enough to go off on my own
To an Action Camp on Mars.

Patricia Leighton

What's in Our Luggage?

Wellies in case it rains,
sunhat for when it's hot,
net for going fishing –
I hope we catch a lot!

Bikes on the roof rack,
bucket and spade for the beach,
marshmallows for toasting –
at least three packets each!

Plasters (I'm bound to fall over!)
sunglasses for when it's bright,
toothbrush (Mum said so),
teddy to cuddle at night.

Picnic on the dashboard
ready for our tea . . .
so much luggage *everywhere*
there's no room left for *me*!

Tracey Blance

Up and About

It's great to be on holiday!
Bet I'm the first one up today...

Big sister's room:
She'll want to play.
She only mumbles,
"Go away!"

Mum and Dad's room:
What do they say?
"It's half past six!
Get up? No way!
Come back in half an hour.
OK?"

But someone's up...
It's Gran. Hooray!
We left the rest to snore away
And went for a walk around the bay.

Eric Finney

Summer Fun

Sunshine,
All's fine.
In car,
Not far.
Park ride,
Seaside.
On sand,
As planned.
Deckchair,
Take care!
Swim wear,
Somewhere.
Don't howl,
Found towel.
Beach clad,
Even Dad.
Beach swim,
Water skim.
One splash,
All dash!
One shout,
All out.
Soaking wet,
No regret.
Water salty,
NOT MY FAULTY!

Awful thirst,
Drink first.
Beach flop,
Lollipop.
Hot feet,
Lunch eat.
Mum burns,
Body turns.
Dad snores,
BOTH BORES!
Sand play,
HOORAY!
Real hassle,
Sandcastle.
Bat, ball,
Sister call.
Run catch,
No match.
Getting late,
Bus waits.
Goodbye,
Sea, sky.
SUMMER FUN,
NUMBER ONE!

Ian Souter

CARtoon

Boot a-bulging, roof rack rocking,
Dad is driving, Katy's coughing,
Mum has migraine, Granny's grumpy,
Baby's bawling (Gran's lap's lumpy).
Sarah swears and sicks up sweeties, Dan the dog is wanting wee-wees.
All around are cars and cases, cones, congestion, furious faces
hauling homeward, slowly, slowly, from a fortnight's (hardly holy!)
"BUMPER B ⬤ onzer Break-A-Way". We never left the m ⬤ torway!

Gina Douthwaite

Snapshots

Families come in many guises
Many shapes and many sizes
But take a good look, and you'll find ME
For I'm the STAR on our family tree.

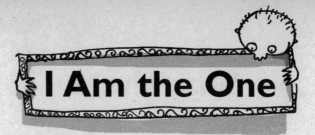

I Am the One

Brilliant

Today Mum called me brilliant
and that's just how I feel

  I'll run a race
    I'm bound to win
  I'll take up golf
    Get a hole in one

Because today Mum called me brilliant
so that's what I must be

  I'll paint a picture
    A work of art
  I'll design a car
    It's sure to start

Because today Mum called me brilliant
and she always speaks the truth

I'll write a song
   It'll be a hit
I'll train a dog
   It'll stand and sit

Because today Mum called me brilliant
Yes, today Mum called me brilliant
   Today Mum called me brilliant
So how am I feeling? BRILLIANT!

Bernard Young

I'm Riding on a Giant

I'm riding on a giant.
I'm way up in the sky.
Looking down on everyone
From higher up than high.

I'm holding on to giant's ears
As we stride along the street
Shouting down at people,
Hey! Mind my giant's feet!

We're ducking down through doorways.
We're walking over walls.
I'm safe as houses way up here
My giant never falls.

People down below us
Simply stop and stare.
Then when they see our shadow,
Oh wow! They get a stare.

I'm taller than the tree-tops
I'm high enough to fly.
Another centimetre and I'd
Bump into the sky.

I've been riding on my giant,
Oh! What a day I've had
I'm not afraid of giants,

'Cause this giant is my dad.

David Whitehead

Old Photos, Old Fashions!

Mum has a photograph of dad
in a purple velvet suit,
a satin tie and green leather shoes,
mum says that he really looked cute!

Dad has a photograph of mum
in a yellow cotton print dress,
a woollen shawl and a pink cloth hat,
mum says that she looked a mess!

Gran has photos of both of them
in the sun on their wedding day.
Mum looked cool in silk and lace
but dad looked hot in flannel grey.

They've all got photographs of me
as a tiny baby looking happy.
My face turns red when I see myself
wearing nothing but a towelling nappy!

Brian Moses

Changing Places

It's strange to think
that my Grandad
is *Dad* to Dad.

When *I'm* a Dad,
will Dad be glad
to be *Grandad*?

Judith Nicholls

Twins in the Family

I'm like her
and she's like me.
We both look like each other.

Our Aunt Sue
is a twin too –
she's the image of my Mother!

With Uncle Jake
it's like a double-take –
my Dad is *his* twin brother!

If we grow up
and we have twins –
we'll be double one another!

John Rice

They Chose Me

I have two mothers,
My birth mother and my Mum.
I have two fathers,
My blood father and my Dad.

But of all the babies born
In the whole wide world
My Mum and Dad chose me.

I have two days,
My Birthday and my Chosen Day.
I get two cakes
And have my friends to tea.

But of all the babies born
In the whole wide world
My Mum and Dad chose me.

I am the one,
The child they went to find,
I am the one
To make their family,

For of all the babies born
In the whole wide world
My Mum and Dad chose me.

Jamila Gavin

Last Word

I'm the Star

Families come in many guises,
Many shapes and many sizes.

First meet the babies, gummy and gooey,
Often wet and *always* pooey,
Then mums and dads, sisters and brothers,
Grans and grandads ... plus a few others.

We're glad they're there, if they weren't we'd
   miss them,
But why? oh why? do we have to *kiss* them?
And the jobs they give us! You wouldn't believe it!
Wash it! Dry it! Tidy and clear it!

Sometimes we get mad (a bit!)
But when we do, they throw a fit.
So mostly we chill out, stay cool,
And let the grown-ups play the fool.

Breakfast ... dinner ... tea ... – I'd say
Meals are the best times of our day.
And when summer comes, if we go away,
We have brilliant times on our holiday.

Families come in many guises,
Many shapes and many sizes,
But take a good look and you'll find ME,
For I'm the STAR on our family tree.

Jennifer Curry

Acknowledgements

The compiler and publishers would like to thank the following for permission to use copyright material in this collection. The publishers have made every effort to contact the copyright holders but there are a few cases where it has not been possible to do so. We would be grateful to hear from anyone who can enable us to contact them so that the omission can be corrected at the first opportunity.

John Agard for "I Din Do Nuttin" from *I Din Do Nuttin* by John Agard pub. Bodley Head. Used by permission of the Random House Group Limited ~ Allan Ahlberg for "Our Mother" from *Please Mrs Butler* by Allan Ahlberg pub. Kestrel, 1983. Copyright © Allan Ahlberg, 1983 ~ Alice Aldous for "When I'm on My Own" from *Wondercrump Poetry*, pub. Red Fox, copyright Random House Children's Books ~ Moira Andrew for "One Parent Family" first published in *A Shooting Star*, ed. Wes Magee, Blackwell, 1985, "A Thoroughly Modern Grandmama" first published in *All in the Family*, ed. John Foster, OUP, 1993, "The Naming Ceremony" first published in *Patchwork of Poems*, ed. Moira Andrew, Belair Publications, 2000 and "My Gran", first published in *Unzip Your Lips*, ed. Paul Cookson, Macmillan, 1998 ~ Tracey Blance for "Home-Time", "The Thing" and "What's in our Luggage?" ~ Valerie Bloom for "Good Advice", from *Let me Touch the Sky* by Valerie Bloom, pub. Macmillan, 2000 ~ Mark Bones for "Beware of the Uncles" and "Grandma's Winter Warmer" ~ Ann Bonner for "Missing Mum" ~ Alexandra Calvert for "Going to Tea with Grandma" from *The Best of Children's Poetry* © Talking Heads Theatre & Poetry ~ Gemma Chilvers for "Birth of a Baby" ~ Moira Clark for "Clickerty-Clackerty High-Heel Song" and "It Isn't Me, Honest" ~ Sue Cowling for "Postcard" ~ Jennifer Curry for "I'm the Star" ~ Gina Douthwaite for "Sisters" and "CARtoon" from *Picture a Poem*, pub. Hutchinson, 1994 ~ Judith Ellis for "Fingerlicking" from *Black Eye Perceptions*, pub. Black Ink, 1981 ~

Eric Finney for "Us", "Mothers' Day", "A Card for Fathers' Day", "I Put My Tongue Out" and "Up and About" and for "The Palindromes", first published in *Crack Another Yolk*, ed. John Foster, OUP, 1996 ~ Jamila Gavin for "They Chose Me" from *Shimmy With My Granny*, ed. Sarah Garland, pub. Hodder Wayland, 1999 ~ Trevor Harvey for "Questions", first published in *Shorts!* ed. Paul Cookson, Macmillan, 2000 ~ Mike Johnson for "Digital Dad" and "Artificial Hip-Hop" ~ Jean Kenward for "Stepmother" ~ Patricia Leighton for "Check the Board", "For Sale", "My Hero", "Unbelievable" and "Holiday Time Again" ~ Wes Magee for "Until Gran Died" and "The Spoons Music Man", both from *The Very Best of Wes Magee*, pub. Macmillan, 2001 ~ Julia Marsden for "Baby Breakfast" from *The Best of Children's Poetry* © Talking Heads Theatre & Poetry ~ Laura Maskell from "A Kid's Life" from *Wondercrump Poetry* pub. Red Fox © Random House Children's Books ~ Glenn Montgomery for "My Brother Barry" from *The Best of Children's Poetry* © Talking Heads Theatre and Poetry ~ Brian Morse for "A Lesson" from *Plenty of Time*, The Bodley Head, 1994. Copyright © Brian Morse, 1994. Reproduced by permission of the author c/o Rogers, Coleridge & White Ltd, 20 Powis Mews, London W11 1JN ~ Brian Moses for "Old Photos, Old Fashions", for "My Little Sister" from *I'm Telling on You* by Brian Moses pub. Macmillan, 1999 and for "Face Pulling Contests" from *Knock Down Ginger & Other Poems* by Brian Moses pub. CUP, 1994 ~ Grace Nichols for "Granny Granny Please Comb My Hair" from *Come Into My Tropical Garden*. Reproduced by permission of Curtis Brown Ltd, London on behalf of Grace Nichols © Grace Nichols, 1988 ~ Judith Nicholls for "Rap-a-Bye Baby", "In Praise of Aunties" and for "Changing Places" from *Someone I Like* by Judith Nicholls, pub. Barefoot Books, 2000. Reprinted by permission of the author ~ Brian Patten for "Squeezes" copyright © Brian Patten, 1985 from *Gargling With Jelly* by Brian Patten, pub. Viking, 1985. Reproduced by permission of the